# Goldilocks and the Three Bears

Illustrated by Dorothea King

Brimax Books Newmarket England

Father Bear, Mother Bear
and Baby Bear lived in
a cottage in the middle of
a wood. Every morning
Mother Bear made porridge
for breakfast. One morning
the porridge was very hot.
"Let us go for a walk while
the porridge cools," said
Father Bear.
The three bears went out into
the sunshine, but forgot to
close the door firmly behind them.

Goldilocks was also out in the
wood that morning. Soon she
came to the bears' cottage.
She saw that the door was open.
Goldilocks peeped inside.
"Is anyone at home?" she
called. Then she noticed
three steaming bowls on the
table and wondered what
was in them. "I will just take
a look," she said. "No one
will know." She tiptoed inside.

When Goldilocks saw the bowls full of porridge, she picked up a spoon.
"I will taste just a little," she said. "No one will know."
She tasted some porridge from the largest bowl. It was too salty. She did not like it.
She tasted some porridge from the middle-size bowl. That was too sweet. She did not like that, either.

By this time Goldilocks was very hungry. She picked up another spoon and tasted some porridge from the smallest bowl. It was not too salty and it was not too sweet. The porridge tasted just right. Because she was a greedy little girl, it was not long before Goldilocks had eaten all of the porridge in the smallest bowl.

Then Goldilocks saw there were three wooden chairs beside the fireplace. Goldilocks decided to try those, too. First she sat in the largest chair. It was too hard. She did not like it. Then she sat in the middle-size chair. That was too soft. She did not like that, either.

Next Goldilocks sat in the smallest chair. It was not too hard and it was not too soft. It felt just right. But the naughty little girl was not right for the smallest chair. She was far too big and heavy and she wriggled about far too much. The little chair broke into pieces and Goldilocks fell to the floor.

Goldilocks picked herself up and went up the winding stairs. There she found three beds, a large one, a middle-size one and a small one. First she sat on the largest bed. It was too hard. She did not like it. Then she sat on the middle-size bed. That was too soft. She did not like that, either.

Next Goldilocks sat on the smallest bed. She found it was not too hard and it was not too soft. The bed was just right. Because she felt so sleepy and because she was such a naughty little girl, Goldilocks curled up tight on the bed and fell fast asleep. She did not hear the three bears returning home.

At once the three bears saw
something was wrong.
"Someone has been eating
my porridge," growled Father
Bear in his loud, gruff voice.
"Someone has been eating
my porridge too," said
Mother Bear in her soft, gruff voice.
"Someone has been eating
my porridge, too," said
in his tiny, gruff voice.
"And they have eaten it all
up." Baby Bear burst into tears.

Mother Bear mopped Baby Bear's tears dry and Father Bear sat down in his chair to think about what was to be done. He jumped up at once in surprise.

"Someone has been sitting in my chair," he growled in his loud, gruff voice.

"Someone has been sitting in my chair, too," said Mother Bear in her soft, gruff voice.

Baby Bear looked sadly at his broken chair.
"Someone has been sitting in my chair," he said in his tiny, gruff voice. "And look, they have broken it into pieces."
Then poor Baby Bear burst into tears for the second time. It made Father Bear and Mother Bear very angry indeed to see Baby Bear cry once more.

Mother Bear dried Baby
Bear's tears, then they all
went upstairs.
"Someone has been lying on
my bed," growled Father
Bear in his loud, gruff voice.
"Someone has been lying on
my bed, too," said Mother
Bear in her soft, gruff voice.
"Someone has been lying on
my bed," said Baby Bear in
his tiny, gruff voice.
"And there she is . . . Look!"

At that moment Goldilocks woke up and saw the three bears. She jumped up, ran down the winding stairs and out of the cottage. She ran all the way home. From then on the three bears closed their cottage door firmly if they went out. They did not want another uninvited guest eating their porridge, breaking their chairs or sleeping in their beds.